THE ENDANGERED

FAMILY

How To Defeat

The Greatest Single Risk

Confronting Your Family

YOUR MONEY

MTM EDUCATIONAL
RESOURCES
For What Matters Most™

By: Monroe "Roey" Diefendorf, Jr.

Shawn T. Barberis

Table of Contents

Forward

If you are one of the fortunate people that has worked hard, become financially successful and accumulated wealth, this book is a practical tool to help keep together what you have put together by preparing your heirs for their "more than money" wealth.

I am not just a proponent of the process espoused in these pages, but our family is a user of the MTM360 technology platform for capturing, protecting and perpetuating our "total" wealth. In addition, after six years of working with the "More Than Money" team of advisors, I am a raving fan.

Whatever your preconceived notions are about money, this book will highlight the implicit dangers that exist with its creation and accumulation, as well as the methodology to mitigate these associated risks.

Do your family a favor and read every word of this book. Take notes, but more importantly, take action! There is a price tag for doing something, but there is an even greater price tag for doing nothing. This new dimension of wealth management has changed the course of our family's trajectory for the better and I only wish I had been introduced to the principles in this book earlier in my life.

I am thankful for the foresight and wisdom that Shawn Barberis and Roey Diefendorf have demonstrated by sharing their lives with our family and now this book with your family.

Cordially,

James

James Webb
Dallas, Texas

Introduction

Being products of the wealth management industry, we were wooed by the sirens of building and preserving wealth and we drank the Kool-Aid that led us, and the others in our cult to believe that "more money is better" (than less money, of course.) But this myopic perspective about money is what is endangering our families from transitioning well from one generation to the next.

Don't get us wrong, wealth creation and preservation is a noble and extremely valuable profession, but the preoccupation of having more money, both for the advisors as well as their clients, fails to address what people want most… a better family.

Having worked with thousands of clients, those with modest assets as well as those with substantial assets, a common theme kept reoccurring – our money is not helping us achieve happiness, nor establishing better relationships, especially among our family. In addition, we found that as the level of assets grew in value, the damage that was inflicted upon one's family also grew – and more money was not the answer.

Finally, we came to a critical point in our careers where we felt it was time to stop the madness and turn the tables on the established wealth management arena. Hence, "More Than Money" wealth management was born and has become our mission. It's a mission that brings family and technology (FamTec) together to address the one's "total" wealth.

This book is a quick read designed to introduce you to our way of thinking and our way of combating the silent killer of our families – the money.

Blessings.

Roey Diefendorf

In the beginning ...

There is a basic tenant in life that revolves around the family being created as the cornerstone of civilization. But that first family illustrates to us that not all ends well when it comes to family. (Adam and Eve's one son, Cain murdered his brother, Abel in a fit of jealousy.) Yet, in the thousands of meetings with clients, not once did the conversation deviate from a desire to care for one's family. Deep rooted within our DNA is family. It is for this reason, that we find it necessary, if not mandatory, to help convey the principles that we have seen benefit families, even those in the midst of turmoil.

But if you are one of those who fail to resonate with "family first," then stop reading now and give this book to someone you believe fits this category.

Money: Friend or Foe

Going back to our Cain and Abel reference, the jealousy and ultimate rage originated in the acceptance by God of their offerings to Him. Abel, a keeper of the sheep, gave the firstlings of his flocks, while Cain, a tiller of the ground gave an offering from his harvest. Cain's offering was rejected by God while Abel's was accepted. Sheep and grain were the currency of the day and so it was their "money" led to the destruction of Abel, their family, and ultimately Cain.

Fast forward to today's currency. We may denominate it in dollars, Euros, etc. or possessions purchased with these currencies, but the bottom line is that "the love of money is the root of all evil." You have it, and I want it. I have it, but I want more.

Money is the lubrication that keeps the engine of our global society moving and without it the engine would seize up. It is a most valuable resource and a tool for families to both survive and thrive on. Money is not the root of all evil. It's when we accumulate wealth that the damage begins to raise its ugly head.

Money is neither friend nor foe. Money is an instrument that wields an enormous amount of power, a force that can build up or tear down. Without a conscious attempt to avert the damage that can be administered, your family is in jeopardy of becoming endangered.

The Inverted U-Shaped World

In 2013, Roey Diefendorf wrote a book entitled, "A Better Way: Using Purposeful Trusts To Perpetuate Your Wealth In Perpetuity." This is an excerpt from that book which describes the dilemma that demands a solution – a "More Than Money" solution.

Chapter 3: Malcolm Gladwell, in his book *David and Goliath,* reasons that we often overlook the obvious to make assumptions that ultimately prove to be incorrect. He uses the biblical story of David and Goliath, along with other examples, to show that unexpected—and often nontraditional—methods can be employed to overcome seemingly insurmountable odds. In the biblical story, David used a stone from his slingshot propelled at 150 miles per hour to strike Goliath in the forehead, dazing him enough to finish the battle at close quarters. Everyone believed small David had no chance against large Goliath—an expectation built on faulty reasoning. In this case, the slingshot is a nontraditional method used to overcome a seemingly overwhelming foe.

Gladwell shows that people in society have many preconceived expectations that are built on faulty reasoning. He relates the story of a California girls basketball team that uses a non-traditional method—a perpetual full-court press—to win against seemingly unbeatable teams and to achieve a "dream season." Again, this is an example of an underdog using a nontraditional approach to solve a difficult problem and achieve an outcome that conflicts with societal expectations.

Gladwell also points out that society generally expects that having more money equates to happiness. However, with respect to raising well-adjusted children, he believes more money only brings happiness to a certain point. He refers to the research of Dr. James Grubman, who has studied the amount of "difficulty" involved in raising well-adjusted children in a wealthy family. Grubman's research indicates that "more is not always better" (going against societal expectations).

And why is this?

According to Grubman, it is due to the fact that we live in an *inverted U-shaped world.*

Gladwell describes an individual who struggles financially as he grows up. He comes from a family that closely watches how they spend every penny. He learns that the family must make value judgments about how to allocate resources. The impact of these struggles during his developmental years is seared into his attitude and behavior patterns. He thus learns the value of money and the virtue of independence and hard work. Yes, we all agree that money is necessary for a "better" life, so he seeks riches to make life easier for his children.

Consider the graph in Figure 3-1, which is derived from a similar graph in *David and Goliath:*

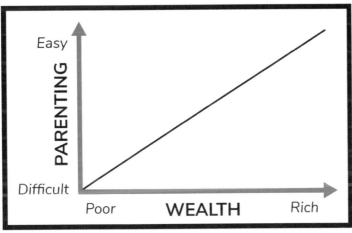

Fig. 3-1

This represents the traditional way of thinking, i.e. that "the more money one has, the easier it will be to raise children." But according to the research of James Grubman, such thinking is based on incorrect data. In fact, the curve should not be linear at all; rather, it should be an inverted U. See Figure 3-2, also derived from David and Goliath, per the ideas of Dr. Grubman. This implies there is a point of diminishing returns—a point where wealth is no longer helpful and ironically becomes hurtful in raising children.

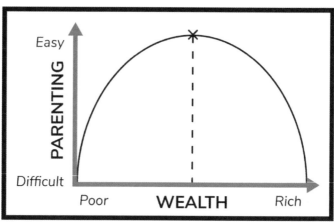

Fig. 3-2

We can use the excellent work of Dr. Grubman, and the insight provided by Malcolm Gladwell in *David and Goliath* as a foundation to build on. According to Grubman, raising children gets more difficult when wealth reaches a certain level. Note that the scale of "difficulty" changes subtly here since the difficulty of not having enough money is different than the difficulty of having too much money. In the former, "difficulty" relates to the inability to provide food and shelter while in the latter, "difficulty" is a measure of something that relates to values (certainly not to an *excess* of food and shelter, the other extreme).

In any case, too much money does create difficulties, and this inverted U-shaped curve illustrates that traditional thinking about wealth creation only works to a certain point. Once one reaches the apex of the curve, "more becomes less." Grubman points out that a family with modest wealth and in the creation stage of their journey, can say "No, we can't" to their children due to lack of resources. However, a family with abundance cannot say "No, we can't" to their children based on a lack of resources; rather, they must say, "No, we *won't*," and this requires a *conversation* with children. Grubman writes that the children need to be taught this message: "Yes, I can buy that for you. But I choose not to. It's not consistent with our values," and this message requires that the parent has a set of values they can articulate and make plausible to the child—very difficult, as Grubman puts it, "under any circumstances and especially if you have a Ferrari in the driveway, a private jet, and a house in Beverly Hills the size of an airplane hangar."

This kind of planning—values-based planning via a purposeful trust—goes far beyond the traditional estate planning and wealth management. It requires that "values" becomes part of the conversation, not simply "valuables."

Based on my experience, I would suggest that in addition to the apex on the inverted U curve, there are two additional points that need to be addressed (see Figure 3-3).

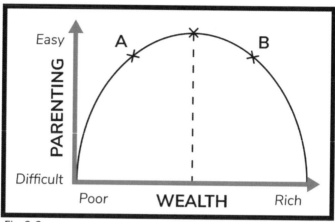

Fig. 3-3

Point B is the point in time when the family realizes that (1) their abundance of wealth has become a problem and (2) that it takes away from the health and "total" wealth of the family. My experience indicates that when a situation reaches this point, it's usually too late— the damage has been done. Point A, on the other hand, occurs when the family has amassed enough wealth and there is still a positive effect on the family from creating more, but the positives come at a diminishing rate. This is the optimal time to initiate values-based planning. Although many would expect that such planning should begin at the apex, for maximum benefit, values-based planning should begin at point A.

The strategies described in "A Better Way" are designed to help you avoid the pitfalls of traditional planning, which all too often lead a family to point B. These strategies will help you plan and implement a new trajectory, one that will allow you to perpetuate values into the next generation. By identifying, articulating your values one can mitigate the negative consequences that traditional planning can bring about.

3D Wealth & "Total" Wealth Management

Having had the benefits of a long career in the financial services industry, my perspective about what wealth is and how to manage it has evolved over time. In 2005, I co-authored with Bob Madden, a book we entitled, "3

Dimensional Wealth: A Radically Sane Perspective on Wealth Management." The premise was "your wealth is more than your money." We refined wealth, developed new paradigms to use wealth, and broadened our focus on how to manage wealth.

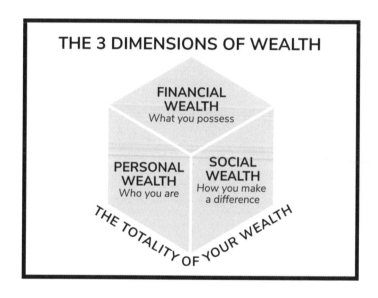

To briefly summarize, we defined wealth in 3 dimensions; personal (who you are), financial (what you have) and social (how to make a difference.) Once you break free from the traditional (1-dimensional) view of your wealth being only your money, then real wealth management can begin.

<u>3 Dimensional Wealth</u>

- Personal Wealth.

- Financial Wealth.

- Social Wealth.

The totality of one's wealth is "more than money."

What Matters Most?

This is THE question that will define how you deal with the remainder of this book.

Allow me to go out on a limb and state that what matters most to most is **FAMILY**. And the desire to provide and care for them often gets translated into a new car, a bigger home, etc., but the money is only one side of the coin.

 Consider one side of the coin as your Financial Wealth (represented by the $ in the illustration below.) However, when we flip over the coin, we find your intangible wealth represented in the illustration as "Family," Life Experiences," and "Philanthropy". And what the researchers are telling us is that the "intangible wealth" is what matters most to families.

THE OTHER SIDE OF THE COIN

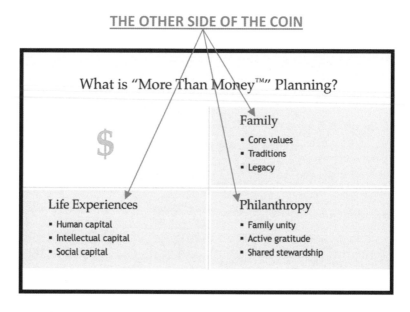

What is "More Than Money™" Planning?

$

Family
- Core values
- Traditions
- Legacy

Life Experiences
- Human capital
- Intellectual capital
- Social capital

Philanthropy
- Family unity
- Active gratitude
- Shared stewardship

The key elements to accomplish family purpose and ideally unity generationally are parents, possessions and purpose. But the greatest of these is purpose.

> ### Three things that keep a family together:
>
> **The Parents**
> (but we all pass away)
>
> **The Possessions**
> (but they dilute/dissipate)
>
> **The Purpose**
> (that perpetuates through the generations)
>
> Family is never done.

Purpose is a rather nebulous word that is kicked around a lot in "legacy" conversations. It is my intention to provide a methodology that will help to articulate your family values (with input from <u>all</u> family members) so that you can pass on your "total" wealth to successor generations.

Because a family's wealth is More Than Money, then to provide for what matters most requires the family to address the other side of the coin – the intangible assets.

The Surveys Say...

Families were surveyed about what they wanted to receive from their parents and grandparents and surprisingly enough it was not valuables related, but values related. Consider the following statistics in the charts below:

70% of all wealth transfers fail in **one generation.**

91% of all wealth transfers fail in **two generations.**

97% of all wealth transfers fail in **three generations.**

The three numbers (70%, 91% & 97%) illustrate the staggering failure rates for keeping together the financial wealth over time.

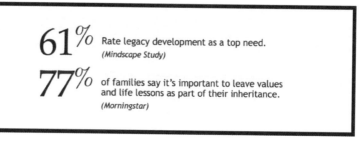

61% Rate legacy development as a top need.
(Mindscape Study)

77% of families say it's important to leave values and life lessons as part of their inheritance.
(Morningstar)

The two numbers (61% & 77%) are what the public desires, and unfortunately is not getting.

So clearly there is a gap from what they want and what they are getting.

And why is that? It's because money (or what money can buy) is not enough to satisfy the soul. Yes, your children are crying out for "more than money" from their family (if you care to listen to them.) Frankly, it's our responsibility to address these wants and needs, to inoculate our children and grandchildren from the silent killer that exists.

What Really Bites You

In another survey, individuals were asked to rank the risks that were most likely to "bite" them. A more interesting set of numbers in the following chart refer to "risk" as perceived by the public.

> **Risk Perception:** *What do I think will bite me?*
>
> **37% investment/asset specific risks**
> Spending risks, business risks, timing risks, portfolio risk, manager risk, style risks...
>
> **26% economy and financial markets risk**
> Economic downturn, inflation, deflation, energy costs, liquidity availability...
>
> **16% tax and political risks**
> Higher personal income taxes and estate taxes, legal liability risks...
>
> ---
>
> **Only 7% of the perceived risk is family dynamics, communication, and lack of a shared purpose.**
> Poor family communication, relationships, engaging the next generation, governance issues...
>
> Source: Family Office Exchange

The three numbers above the line (37%, 26% & 16%, which were ranked by highest response rates, totaling 79%), all referred to risk in basically financial terms.

The one number below the line showed that people had an extremely low perception of risk (7%) due to family dynamics (non-financial).

Contrast these results with the <u>actual</u> results from the Williams & Pressier study that follows.

> **Risk Reality:** *What bit me?*
>
> **60% of failure** is due to a lack of communication and trust within the family around group decision making, shared purpose, education and governance.
>
> **25% of failure** is due to unprepared/disengaged heirs.
>
> ---
>
> **Only 3% of failure is due to failures in financial planning, taxes and investments!**
>
> Source: Williams and Pressier

The highest real risks came from family dynamics and only 3% of the wealth transfer failures came from financial, tax and investments.

Here's the problem: the financial world spends most of its time creating solutions to problems that don't exist. Isn't it time we turn things upside down and spend time on what matters most and where the best results will be achieved?

If your advisors neglect your family dynamics in their discussion of your "total" wealth, then most of your efforts are for naught.

And we do this, generation after generation, and come up with the statistics outlined above.

It's time to be break this destructive cycle.

Are you shocked to learn that 85% of the time it is the non-financial issues that cause the majority of the damage to your family?

The Silent Killer

There is a saying that says, "shirt sleeves to shirt sleeves in three generations." The first generation earns the wealth, the second generation lives off the wealth and the third generation squanders the wealth. And this goes on century after century, and no one culture or ethnic peoples are exempt. Failure is the word that comes to mind.

It's much like Dr. Frankenstein who spends his life working on making a living being, only to ultimately find that his creation is the thing that destroys him.

In the context of family, what does "fail" mean?

The Definition of Fail

Net worth is depleted.
Financial security disappears (regardless of the fantastic job you do creating it for them).

Intangible assets are slowly forgotten.
Diminished or no legacy (how many of you know your grandparent's first names or their occupation?)

Family unity is fractured.
Disharmony, resentment, legal battles (read the newspapers lately?)

Yes, the thing that we so much wanted to be healthy (our families) we now find are doomed to fail. This destructive "thing" is so subtle and deceptive to our consciousness that it goes undetected and therefore unattended until such time that the cure is insufficient to remedy the situation.

What is this silent killer? It's your money. Yes, the very item that you spend all your time discussing and strategizing with your professional advisors is not the cure to your family's failure, but indeed the cause.

Let's unpack this thought a little more.

Putting it All Together

Once you have identified and acknowledged that your wealth is truly "more than money" you need a methodology to synchronize the 3 dimensions of your wealth.

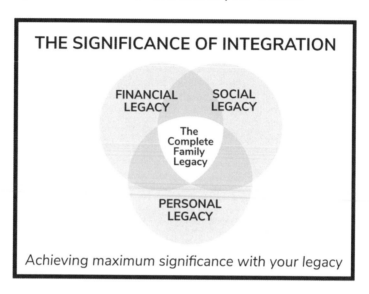

THE SIGNIFICANCE OF INTEGRATION

FINANCIAL LEGACY

SOCIAL LEGACY

The Complete Family Legacy

PERSONAL LEGACY

Achieving maximum significance with your legacy

We are assuming that you have had ample opportunity to work on your Financial Wealth with your advisors. But how do you transition into a discussion of Personal and Social Wealth and incorporate them into your "total" wealth plan?

First, it is important to find advisors who are equipped to address these other intangible dimensions of your wealth.

Next, it is important to make your family part or your total wealth plan.

Our experience has proven over and over that by providing our clients this expanded view of wealth that the family unit is strengthened.

What comes next is the critical pivotal link from financial to family.

The Starting Point: Modern Portfolio Theory (MPT)

In 1952, Harry Moskowitz published his paper, "Portfolio Selection," in the Journal of Finance. Markowitz was considered the father of modern portfolio theory and was awarded a Nobel prize for developing MPT.

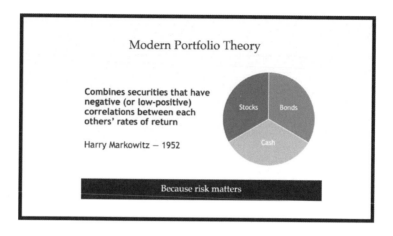

Markowitz used mathematics to explain the relationship of risk to return as it relates to asset allocation. He proved that asset classes acted differently during a market cycle and discussed how portfolios could be constructed to match investor risk tolerance and expected returns. The objective was to ultimately select a group of investment assets which collectively lowered risk more than any single asset on its own.

MPT argues that an investment's risk and return characteristics should <u>not be viewed alone</u> but should be evaluated by how the investment affects the overall portfolio risk and return.

MPT shows that an investor can construct a portfolio of multiple assets that will maximize returns for a given level of risk. Likewise, given a desired level of expected return, an investor can construct a portfolio with the lowest possible risk. One individual investment's return is less important than how the investment behaves in the context of the entire portfolio.

MPT has become the tool which explains how to find the best possible diversification strategy. Some 67 years later, this remains the foundation for investment portfolio construction.

Family as an Asset Class

What if it were possible to add an Intangible asset, such as family, into the mix with the tangible assets, such as stocks, bonds and cash?

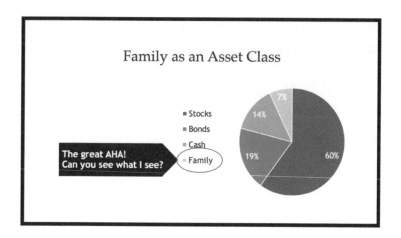

If we can re-define wealth into 3 dimensions, then it is plausible to re-define asset allocation by expanding Modern Portfolio Theory (MPT) into 3D Portfolio Theory (3DPT). MPT is a great tool to minimize the risk in your financial wealth and keep together what you have put together monetarily. But 3DPT is the tool to keep together what God has put together – your family.

An Overview: 3 Dimensional Portfolio Theory (3DPT)

If we add a 3 dimensional view to Modern Portfolio Theory, this suggests that one could create a portfolio that could, and should, include "more than money".

I believe that this broadened view of MPT is the holy grail that makes Markowitz Nobel work take on even greater meaning.

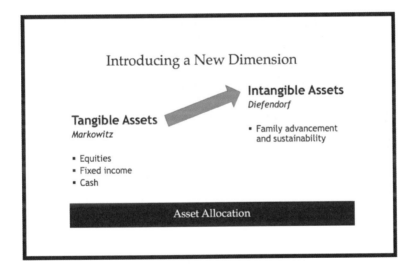

3 Dimensional Portfolio Theory (3DPT) is the way for a family to mitigate the risk associated with transferring wealth from one generation to another, by introducing a

"more than money" asset class into the family's asset allocation.

While there is no mathematical formula associated with incorporating "values" into the "values" mix, studies have shown that without the family addressing values, gratitude, legacy and governance, there is an increased risk of the family wealth being lost in only three generations.

A New Asset Class: Family Advancement & Sustainability

One of the premises of 3DPT, is that there must be a new asset class created to add to the traditional mix. This asset class represents the intangible wealth that comes from your family and your family values. It is like going to a 3D movie and putting on those funny looking glasses. Once on your face and the movie rolls, you see things in a totally different perspective.

Hence, we have created the "Family Advancement & Sustainability" (FAS) asset classification. The meaning of FAS can be ascertained by looking at each word separately.

- **Family** – This indicates that this is not something that can be accomplished or achieved individually but requires the participation of multiple individuals over multi-generations.
- **Advancement** – This refers to a process that is well thought out and choreographed to prepare the heirs for what lies ahead.
- **Sustainability** – This is achieved by hard work on the part of a family so that both the "values" and "valuables" are perpetuated and preserved for generations to come.

Preparing one's heirs is the critical factor in the perpetuation of a family's "total" wealth for generations to come. This process has been compared to the "exchange zone" as it relates to running (and winning) a relay race and preparing heirs for the ultimate handoff of wealth from one generation to the next. Allow me to summarize in my own words.

In the 2008 Summer Olympics, the USA was winning the 4x4 men's relay race when on the transfer of the baton, it was dropped, and the race was lost. Bottom line is that it is not how fast you run the race, but how well you perform the handoff.

This is true in transferring wealth from one generation to the next. It is not how fast you accumulate money (the assumption being that a better return on investment will get you "there" faster) or how much you accumulate (the assumption is the more you have the more can be left behind), but rather how well you pass the baton (prepare your heirs for their wealth.)

It is remarkably interesting how much time and effort is spent by relay teams on choreographing and rehearsing the "exchange zone." In fact, there are six phases to the transfer of the baton. From a potential baton recipient standing still, to getting started, to hitting their full speed and ultimately receiving the baton at which time the former runner falls back into the distance.

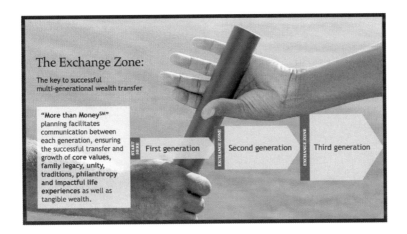

The Exchange Zone:

The key to successful multi-generational wealth transfer

"More than Money^{SM}" planning facilitates communication between each generation, ensuring the successful transfer and growth of core values, family legacy, unity, traditions, philanthropy and impactful life experiences as well as tangible wealth.

First generation | Second generation | Third generation

I suggest there exists a well thought out process that a family can choreograph and rehearse so that when it is time for the transfer of wealth, the exchange is successful. This exchange zone for multi-generation wealth transfer is what we call "family advancement & sustainability." Without this purposeful addition to the wealth transfer process, you and your family will become one of the statistics, most likely.

Rather than leaving your wealth transfer to chance, lets incorporate the tools available to do it right (and you only have one chance to do it right.)

You've prepared the money for the family, but...
have you prepared the family for the money?

3DPT In Action: Integrating FAS Into Portfolio Management

When we add FAS to the array of equity allocations (large cap, small cap, international, etc.) and fixed income (long term, short term, corporate, etc.), this means that any allocation towards FAS will have to reduce the existing allocations within one's portfolio.

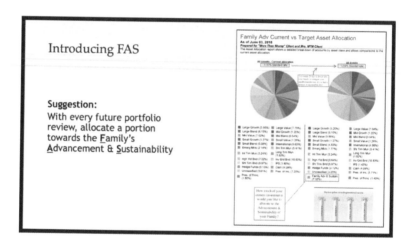

But remember, an allocation towards preparing heirs mitigates the risk in the family's wealth transfer, so this should be a <u>required allocation in EVERY investment portfolio</u>. Ignoring its importance and benefit to the family you counsel, would be tantamount to malpractice. It is imperative that advisors prepare themselves to guide their clients and their families through the exchange zone. In our practice, we have incorporated into our asset allocation software, (we use e-Money,) the FAS asset class and assign a percentage of the portfolio F/B/O the family. In the following example, we have recommended a target allocation of 7.52% towards FAS.

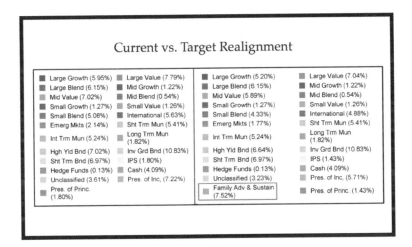

When we hit the rebalancing button (a robo function), the current vs. target portfolio indicates that we must decrease the weightings into the other asset classes and the reduction in the return on the assets goes down from 6.93% to 6.64%. In other words, for 29 basis points reduction in returns, you could implement the Family Advancement & Sustainability program for preparing heirs.

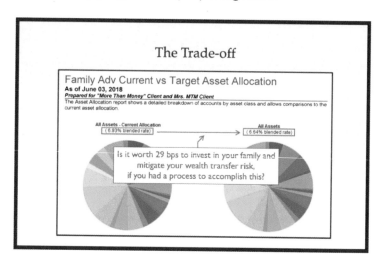

In all my career, I have never had a client say, "Roey, what I would really like is another 29 bps return on my investments." What I do hear them say is," I don't want my children to fight over our money. I'm concerned about the damage that my money might do to our kids." It's not that they want less money (as they are concerned about making sure that their money is working for them), but what they genuinely want is all about "more than money."

So rather than have the interest and dividends from the 7.52% allocation of investments be reinvested to make more money, we use the dividends and interest to institute a program with their family that is about "more than money."

This subtle <u>redirection of assets</u> is monumental in the impact that it can have. It's the shift from preparing the money for the heirs, to preparing the heirs for the money.

The four pillars upon which the family's preparation centers around are:

- Values
- Legacy
- Gratitude
- Governance

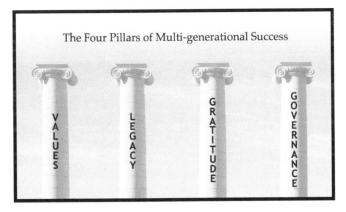

The Four Pillars of Multi-generational Success

Each of these provides the fertile soil required to grow strong roots in their family tree. The goal is to "build a better family."

(Note: Families are made up of flawed individuals, thus family dynamics are messy. But rather than throw up our hands and say, "there is really nothing we can do," it is worth attempting to work hard to perpetuate the family's "total" wealth for generations to come.)

The Mechanics: Dividend Investment vs. Reinvestment

Once it is determined that an allocation towards "family" is a desired goal, then how do we accomplish putting meat on the bones?

Our new re-balancing into Family Advancement & Sustainability will give the family "permission" to allocate resources to prepare their heirs.

For our advisory firm, this FAS allocation provides ample income to pay for:

1. The Annual Family Forum, plus
2. The MTM360 digital process led by an experienced MTM Advisor, and upon request

3. The MTM Advisor's facilitation at the Family Forum.

Let me walk you through an example of how this works. Let's work backwards. In order to have an effective "exchange zone" in the wealth transfer process, there needs to be ample time for real discussion – a guided discussion around the four foundational pillars. In most of the families we work with, this extended period they spend together is their family vacation. This can be as simple as a weekend away or an extended trip to an exotic location. But whatever the cost associated with this family activity, we guestimate what that might be. Let's assume in this example that this family vacation cost approximately $30,000 per year. And if we assume that we generate a 6.0% return on investment after taxes and fees, it will require an allocation of $500,000. That's Step One.

Next, we determine how much our advisory fee would be to navigate the family through the four foundational pillars. This is dependent upon the number of family members that will be participating in the program. At our advisory firm, we charge $5,000 per family portal. So, a family of mom and dad, with 3 adult children (total of 5), would total $25,000 (5 X $5,000). Again, if we assume that we generate a 6.0% return on investment after taxes and fees, it will require an allocation of $416,666. That's Step Two.

Finally, when the family desires an MTM Advisor to be present at their Family Forum, we bill a daily flat rate, plus travel.

Let's summarize, the allocation of capital required to fund both Step 1 and Step 2.

Step 1 - $500,000 of capital would be allocated to pay for their Family Forum, however remember, they are already paying for their family vacation, so this allocation is not required at this time.

Step 2 - $416,666 of capital allocated for the payment of MTM Advisory fees on assets of $5,540,771 equals a 7.52% weighting into the FAS asset class.

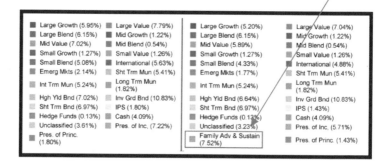

That's the easy part. The real question is, "How do we navigate a family through the four foundational pillars?

Family + Technology: "FamTec"

With "FinTech" taking all the headlines, the time has come for the madness to stop. More money is not the answer. Hence, we coined the term: Family + Technology (FamTec), a concept whose time has come. Granted, this is truly swimming against the tide, as the large financial institutions measure their success by the assets under management, and so for them, more is better. But I believe that this approach is naïve and worse yet, dangerous.

So, this begs the question, can technology really help "build a better family?" With over 50% of nuclear families crumbling and extended families spread all over the

Trust me when I say "FamTec" is going to become mainstream.

globe, can technology work to improve the "total" wealth transfer results?

The answer is "yes."

Asset Allocation: "FinTech"

A day does not go by when we are reading about the virtues of Financial Technology ("FinTech"), providing faster, better, cheaper solutions to our portfolio needs. And this is quite true. In our own asset management division, we are always seeking to find new ways to make our lives easier, particularly in the area of asset allocation.

"FinTech" has changed the landscape of wealth management by commoditizing our services. For decades, we have been providing re-balancing of our client's portfolios which has been part of our fee for service. Now "Alexa" can re-balance your portfolio while you are brushing your teeth (if she can understand you with your mouth full.)

So, in the context of MPT, where we seek to dampen volatility through diversification, asset allocation is no longer only for those who are "paying attention" (and paying a fee). What Harry Markowitz set out to achieve is a viable solution to all, thanks to technology.

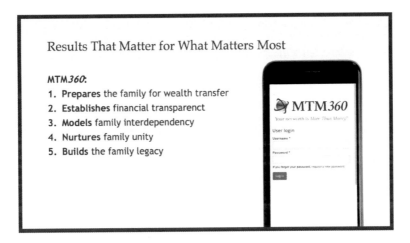

If your family is going to speak the language of the NextGen, then it is going to require a digital tool. FamTec is the "hot dot" to follow.

MoreThanMoney360: Digital Multi-generational Tool

Roey Diefendorf has been a man on a mission for over 15 years, working to create tools that will help me become a better "total" wealth manager. It wasn't until 2016, he teamed up with Shawn Barberis, that they put together the digital platform for addressing the four foundational pillars in successful multi-generational transfers: values, gratitude, legacy and governance.

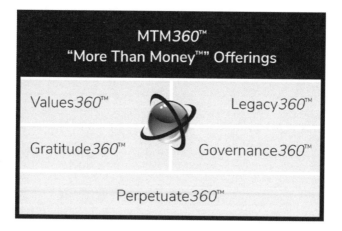

It is a time efficient, guided, digital system to prepare families for multi-generational success.

This is a key part of connecting the dots; going from thought to finish. It's wonderful to allocate resources to FAS, but where does a family start on the journey and what resources will the journey require and how do we know we are on the right path?

MoreThanMoney360 (MTM360) is <u>THE</u> digital tool that allows all family members to "be heard" and provide input into a data base where the results are aggregated for the family to provide data points for having meaningful guided conversations at the "Family Forums."

Right from the palm or your hand, a family can share insights about "what matters most" in preparation for a Family Forum.

To successfully prepare your heirs, please note that the Family Forum is <u>not optional</u>. It is the where the "magic" happens and is comprised of three elements;

- Fun, Education, and Governance.

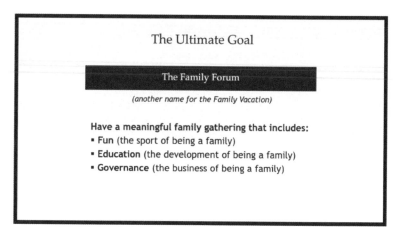

Each Family Forum revolves around one of the four foundational pillars. MTM360 is broken into four projects, each include five deliverables at each family forum.

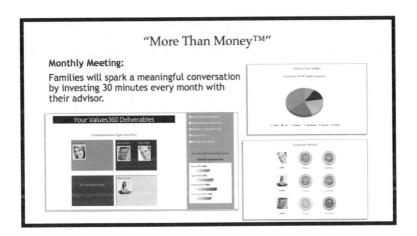

The key to the success of preparing heirs is meaningful communication within the family. This integration of "values" with "valuables" is the combination for growing and sustaining a family's "total" wealth for generations.

Technology for Empowering Families

To learn more about these projects you can go to www.MoreThanMoney360 .com.

The Endowment: Family Advancement & Sustainability Trust (FAST)

Colleges and universities have learned that the key to their viability is to create an endowment; a pool of capital whose income generating properties fund the ongoing day to day expenses. In fact, so vital is this component in the sustainability of these institutions that they place a great emphasis on the solicitation of donors to become these patrons. And many families have accepted the call and have endowed university chairs.

The Family Advancement & Sustainability Trust

"Parents are more likely to endow a chair at a university to help educate strangers than to endow a chair at their Family Table to help educate the family."

—Tom Rogerson

How do you endow a chair at your family table designed to **invest into** your family members rather than **distribute to** your family members?

A friend of mine, Tom Rogerson along with Marvin Blum and Gary Post have written an article that was published in Trust & Estates Magazine in October 2018. The premise is that the allocation of resources that we previously discussed towards the Family Advancement & Sustainability deserves to be endowed for generations.

This type of trust differs from others because the beneficiary does not receive distributions to be spent on their own personal values. Rather, the trust distributions are used to perpetuate the values of the grantor; in other words, preparing the heirs for the money.

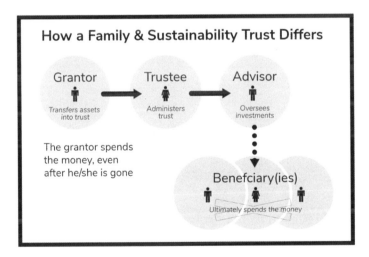

Let's refer to our earlier example on page 43 of the allocation of capital required to fund both Step 1 and Step

2 in FAS asset class. The distinction here is that for the Family Forum to continue, it must be funded.

Step 1 - $500.000 of capital would be allocated to pay for their Family Forum.

Step 2 - $416,667 of capital allocated to pay for the MTM Advisory fees.

Step 3 - $83,333 of capital would be ample to pay the corporate trustee fees for a dynasty trust.

How do you determine the allocation toward your FAST?		
3 components to your FAST	Sample annual expense	Required capital
A. The Family Forum	$ 30,000	$ 500,000
B. The MTM360 Digital Platform with MTM Navigator	$ 25,000	$ 416,667
C. SD Dynasty Trustee Fees	$ 5,000	$ 83,333
Projected ROI 6.00%	Annual distribution for your FAST	Required to endow your FAST
	$ 60,000	$ 1,000,000

This means that the total capital is the sum of 1, 2 & 3, or $1,000,000.

By funding the FAST in one lump sum, this one decision will assure that your family will not have to make annual decisions as to whether to continue engaging the family unit within the Family Forum construct.

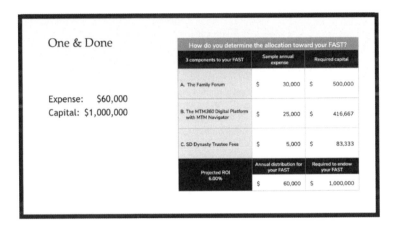

One & Done

Expense: $60,000
Capital: $1,000,000

How do you determine the allocation toward your FAST?		
3 components to your FAST	Sample annual expense	Required capital
A. The Family Forum	$ 30,000	$ 500,000
B. The MTM360 Digital Platform with MTM Navigator	$ 25,000	$ 416,667
C. SD Dynasty Trustee Fees	$ 5,000	$ 83,333
Projected ROI 6.00%	Annual distribution for your FAST	Required to endow your FAST
	$ 60,000	$ 1,000,000

Two Phases To The FAST: Legacy Creation & Perpetuation

In the <u>Legacy Creation Phase</u>, there are two funding sources: People @ Work and Money @ Work. What we have found is that most families will fund their Family

Forum – Step 1 (their family vacation with a purpose) out of their earned income. This leaves only Step 2 to fund from their assets.

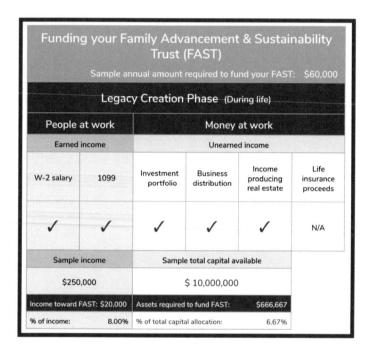

Funding your Family Advancement & Sustainability Trust (FAST)					
Sample annual amount required to fund your FAST: $60,000					
Legacy Creation Phase (During life)					
People at work		Money at work			
Earned income		Unearned income			
W-2 salary	1099	Investment portfolio	Business distribution	Income producing real estate	Life insurance proceeds
✓	✓	✓	✓	✓	N/A
Sample income		Sample total capital available			
$250,000		$ 10,000,000			
Income toward FAST: $20,000		Assets required to fund FAST:		$666,667	
% of income:	8.00%	% of total capital allocation:		6.67%	

In order to perpetuate the ongoing process after death, it can be done by increasing the allocation towards the FAS or one can take an "option" for the remainder of the endowment. This means securing a life insurance policy within the trust to fund Step 1 at the death of the grantor.

At death, the only way to fund a FAS is through "Money @ Work." It is important to understand that funding is not limited to one's investment portfolio managed by an investment advisor.

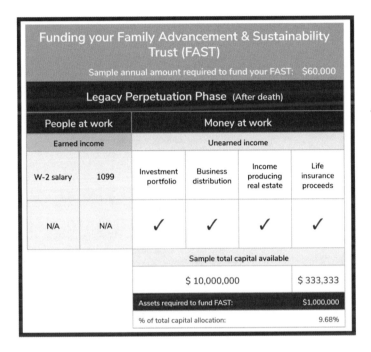

All assets (investment portfolio, business distributions, income producing real estate and life insurance proceeds) can be used to fund the FAS.

During the Legacy Perpetuation Phase the ultimate objective to assure sustainability is to create a "South Dakota, Directed, Asset protection, Dynasty" Trust to endow the MTM360 process. This becomes the true foundational element for the family to rely on for funding for generations.

The following flowchart illustrates how the various moving pieces work together.

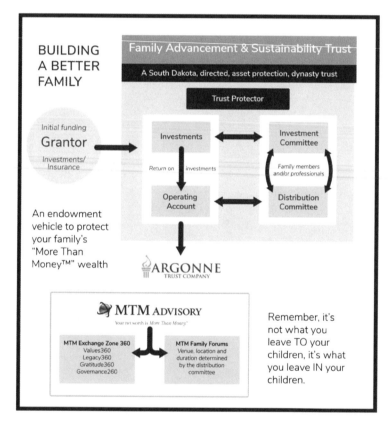

A Review: FinTech/FamTec Summary

When Financial Technology and Family Technology meet and work together, the results will be extremely rewarding as an advisor, as well as for the family.

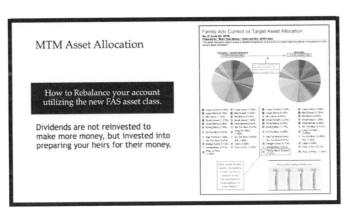

Let's review what's going on with 3D Portfolio Theory.

1) 3DPT is a process to mitigate the risk associated with multi-generational wealth transfer failures.
2) A new asset class is created; Family Advancement & Sustainability (FAS) and incorporated into your FinTech asset allocation software.
3) It introduces the MTM360 digital platform for advisors to serve families.
4) FinTech incorporates asset allocation for funding the FamTec solution.
5) The Family Advancement & Sustainability Trust (FAST) endows the MTM360 process.

MPT was the award-winning financial wealth risk mitigation tool for the 20th century, but as we moved into the 21st century 3DPT will hopefully gain traction with not only families but with the Goliath financial institutions.

Reverse The Flow

In October 1871 Chicago Fire destroyed much of the city. Surprisingly, the fire started on the other side of the Chicago River. So how did the flames cross the river and cause such great distraction? This river jumping fire is partially explained by the wooden ships that were moored in the Chicago River as the fire would have travel that way, but there is also another even more important factor in the spread of the fire. In those days, the Chicago River was a shallow sluggish sewer for the entire city. The Union Stockyards in Chicago would dump all the animal waste into the river and people referred to it as "the stinking river." It was so bad that the waste was actually combustible. All this decay flowed into Lake Michigan where there were drinking water intakes for the city. And waterborne diseases naturally broke out because of it. Every year throughout the 1880's and 1890's at least 10,000 people died from cholera and the typhoid fever. In 1885, fourteen years after the great Chicago Fire, nearly 100,000 people died from illnesses carried by the river's putrid waters. Finally, city engineers decided to do something, and they started digging 28 miles of canals. They moved more earth and rocks than was taken to build the Panama Canal. They set locks and gates in place and then on January 2, 1900, a worker opened a drain gate allowing Lake Michigan and the other Great Lakes to flow into the Chicago River, pushing it in a direction it had never flowed before. They reversed the flow of the Chicago River. It flowed the opposite way, into the canal, into the Des Plaines River, into the Illinois River and then into the Mississippi River. This brought a huge flow of fresh water and instead of shallow, sluggish diseased water making the community sick, the river now brought the city life. Some argue that the city of Chicago would not exist today if the flow of the river has not been reversed.

What is needed today is a reengineering of wealth management to reverse the flow of "more money" as the financial industry's prescription for individuals and families. Similar, to the Chicago River, money alone can become a fire accelerant vs. a fire retardant. Without an inflow of "more than money" into the wealth management mix, the money by itself can become toxic.

Evolution or Revolution?

From More Money to More Than Money.

Roey Diefendorf was the 4th generation in a life insurance dynasty that began in 1875. With the changes that have occurred over the past 144 years, we have had to adapt to survive. In the late 1800's life expectancy was age 47, hence retirement planning was non-existent. Compare that to today and what is just around the corner. I have heard it said that if you live to 2030, you have an excellent chance of living to age 110. Portfolio construction is paramount to financial independence. But is there more to portfolio construction than economics? Perhaps there are those that will think this is too far off the beaten path of wealth management. But all I ask is that keep an open mind and come to your own conclusion. Note: I am "swimming upstream" as the flow of funds from the financial giants seem to say, "more money is better." This is not true if you are interested in "building a better family."

MoreThanMoney360 is the total wealth risk mitigation tool of the future as we look towards the 22nd century.

"FAMILY IS NEVER DONE"

Appendix

A: FAST -Trusts & Estates – December 2017

FEATURE:
THE MODERN PRACTICE

By **Marvin E. Blum, Gary V. Post and Thomas Rogerson**

A FAST Solution to Legacy Planning

The "family advancement sustainability trust"

In their recent article entitled, "Innovate or Die," Timothy J. Belber, Ian McDermott, and John A. Warnick assess the current estate-planning landscape and perceptively find the profession to be at a turning point.[1] While tactical, tax-driven planning (along with asset protection planning) was the driving force for estate planning throughout the 1980s, 1990s and early 2000s, the authors point out that there are forces at work disrupting the traditional paradigm of tax-centered estate planning. The passage of the American Taxpayer Relief Act of 2012 and its increased exemptions, higher income tax rates and portability may have triggered a renewed emphasis on technical estate-planning practices, but a number of societal changes are placing a new demand on estate planners. There's a chasm developing between what constitutes a traditional estate plan and what clients need and expect. Belber, McDermott and Warnick make it clear that estate planners must address these new developments or run the risk of becoming obsolete.

For those seeking to stay ahead of the changing landscape, the first step is an understanding of the ways in which traditional estate planning falls short of meeting a client's needs. The problem with traditional planning is that it's far too narrow in its scope. Historically, an expertly crafted estate plan would transfer wealth from one generation to the next in a tax-efficient manner,

From left to right **Marvin E. Blum** is the founder and **Gary V. Post** is a partner, both at The Blum Firm, P.C., in Fort Worth, Texas. **Thomas Rogerson** is a family wealth

strategist at Wilmington Trust in Wilmington, Del.

protecting the client's assets and ensuring an effective system was in place to administer those assets for heirs. While this process remains the foundation of estate planning, it's become only the first part of a two-part race. More and more, clients are beginning to understand that even the most well-crafted estate plan will be useless if it fails to address their qualitative goals and/or if their heirs are unprepared to receive the inheritance. The innovative, adaptive estate-planning attorney will break from the confines of the traditional model to include "expanded planning" as the second part of the estate-planning process.

Two-Stage Process

Stage 1: This stage is twofold: (1) begin the process of teaching and enhancing family communication skills, and (2) work with family members and spouses at the first generation (G1) and second generation (G2) levels (and third generation (G3) if practical) to clarify and commit to family beliefs, shared values and goals. The ultimate objective of this first stage is to create a collective family mission statement outlining the family's core values, beliefs and goals. This process can yield three useful results for moving to the next level of expanded planning.

1. Start the ongoing process of garnering participation and buy-in from G1, G2 and G3 (if practical), building cohesion and connection and giving the family members a cause behind which they can unite.

2. Identify relationship issues that can be addressed and resolved while the matriarch and patriarch are alive and participating. Relationship issues can spring from obvious situations such as a family business, a second marriage or access, use and management of a family ranch or vacation home. Further, the process

can identify subtle, yet important, conflicts among family members that can emerge as a disruptive influence on family harmony if not identified and resolved while G1 is still living.

3. The family mission will be the springboard from which will emerge the estate plan for the family. The mission will drive the estate plan, and the estate plan will in turn be structured to support the mission.

Stage 2: Build and implement the family estate plan. Planning under the expanded model will differ from the traditional system in two primary ways. First, the

Structurally, a FAST is a standard dynasty trust, but with a spin— it's a directed trust created in Delaware or a state with similar directed trust laws.

plan will be purpose-driven and tailored to the family in that its purpose will be to advance the values, beliefs and goals set forth in the family mission statement. Second, the plan will be beneficiary-focused and oriented toward ensuring a family's wealth exists for more than one generation.

Tools to Implement Plan

With these parameters of the expanded planning model in place, the question remaining is what tools will be used to implement and operate the plan on an ongoing basis. For this, it's helpful to look to successful multi-generational families as models. No two families are the same, but through the use of concepts such as family retreats, educational development and organized governance, families who've managed to skirt the old "shirtsleeves-to-shirtsleeves" adage provide a template of best practices to incorporate into a client's expanded planning. For some estate planners, the idea of expanded planning may seem too abstract. Often, the concepts

may be easy to discuss with the client but ultimately become too difficult to implement, which is why it's necessary for planners to have a practical tool available to help achieve the objectives of expanded planning. One such tool is a family advancement sustainability trust (FAST), a new type of trust that essentially serves as the legs of expanded planning, providing both the money to fund planning strategies and the leadership to place those strategies into motion.[1] It isn't enough for G1 to implement best practices and just hope that the family will continue them. To beat the odds and overcome the "shirtsleeves" adage, G1 needs to put a structure in place. For example, when G1 is gone, G2 (or their spouses) may resist paying for their portion of the family retreats out of their pocket. Once G1 creates a FAST and funds it, the FAST can provide the funds to pay for the retreat, and one of the FAST's decision-making bodies is charged with the responsibility of making sure the retreat actually happens.

The FAST

To appreciate how a FAST facilitates expanded planning, it's first necessary to understand the technical nuts and bolts of what a FAST is. At its core, the FAST is created to support the institution of the family, investing in family members rather than simply distributing assets to heirs. Structurally, a FAST is a standard dynasty trust, but with a spin—it's a directed trust created in Delaware or a state with similar directed trust laws. With a directed trust, decision-making authority isn't concentrated solely in the trustee, but instead can be split among one or more advisors to the trust. Specifically, decisions regarding administrative matters, trust investments and trust distributions may be assigned to separate co-trustees, advisors or trust protectors. Thus, the significance of the directed trust is that it allows family members and trusted advisors of the family to directly participate in the governance of the trust.

Accordingly, a FAST contains four decision-making bodies, described in detail below. Individuals may serve on more than one committee, and non-family committee members receive compensation for serving on a committee. The grantor(s) would likely desire to be a member of each committee.

Four Decision-Making Bodies

1. **Administrative trustee.** Typically, a corporate trustee serves as the administrative trustee. The

administrative trustee has no control over investment or distribution decisions but rather deals strictly with generic trust-related tasks such as recordkeeping and maintaining custody of the trust's assets.

2. **Investment committee.** The investment committee is commonly comprised of three members: two family members and one professional advisor. The professional advisor could be a peer, such as a family investment advisor or some other type of fiduciary, or could be a hired investment advisor. The investment committee is charged with making all decisions relating to the investment of trust assets.

3. **Distribution committee.** The distribution committee is comprised of several members, for example two family members, a professional consultant who has experience working with families on legacy planning, an individual who's a like-minded peer to the grantor and one other advisor (family attorney or accountant) with professional expertise who also brings a knowledge of or familiarity with the family. A key aspect of the FAST is that the responsibilities of the distribution committee are much broader than in typical trusts. Whereas in other trusts, a distribution committee makes decisions regarding the disbursement of trust assets, in a FAST, the distribution committee is charged with spending trust assets to preserve and strengthen the family institution.

4. **Trust protector committee.** The trust protector committee may be comprised of three professional members such as the family's attorney, CPA, financial advisor and/or a trusted fiduciary. Although it wouldn't be advisable to have a family member serve on the trust protector committee, family members could serve as consultants to the committee. The trust protectors are individuals charged with playing the role of the grantor once the grantor is no longer able to do so. Some typical trust protector duties include removing or appointing trustees, committee members or other advisors and amending the governing instrument of the trust to efficiently administer the trust or to achieve favorable tax status for the trust.

As noted above, a key component of the FAST is that it allows family members and trusted advisors of the family to directly participate in the governance of the trust. A way to be sure these fiduciaries are accountable to carry out the tasks that have been assigned to them is to include a peer review process in the FAST to be administered by the trust protector committee. Within the context of trusts, peer review is a tool used solely as a positive review process of trust operations. Essentially, peer review is a way for an objective person or committee to perform a check-up on how well the trust is continuing to meet the patriarch's and matriarch's original objectives. As such, it's a healthy way to assure the patriarch and matriarch that the long-term stability and effectiveness of the trust will continue to be monitored. A peer review system requires careful thought and drafting. The trust agreement should include a requirement that the review occur periodically. The reviewers should be objective and unbiased and should receive reasonable compensation for their efforts and expenses. Although peer reviewers have no enforcement authority, their reports act as checks on the committees and can provide clients with the assurance of knowing that as younger generations become committee members, they won't be without continued guidance.

> It's important to consider when to create and how to fund the FAST.

Creation and Funding

It's important to consider when to create and how to fund the FAST. Creating a FAST should ideally occur during the patriarch's and matriarch's lifetimes to allow G1 to mold the trust to reflect the needs and ideals of the family. Moreover, initiating operation of a FAST during the lifetime of G1 helps to guide family members and advisors and establish the direction of the FAST for future generations.

The FAST may be minimally funded during the lifetimes of G1, with additional funds contributed to the trust on their deaths. The amount of funding can be either a fixed amount or a percentage of the estate. It will vary from family to family according to their means and the FAST's agenda. During the patriarch's and matriarch's lifetimes, FAST-related activities such as family retreats and educational programs can be paid for either out of G1's pocket or from the FAST.

Although there are several ways to fund a FAST, two primary funding techniques are the special purpose irrevocable life insurance trust (ILIT) and the 678 trust (also known as a "beneficiary defective irrevocable trust" or "BDIT"). With a special purpose ILIT, a stand-alone ILIT holds a life insurance policy on the patriarch or matriarch that funnels additional funds into the FAST at the death of G1. The other funding technique involves the use of a 678 trust, which is a unique estate-planning tool that allows clients to combine asset protection,

> The FAST aims to provide practical experience by serving as a mentor to beneficiaries, imparting wisdom instead of simply acting as a gatekeeper to the family wealth

estate tax savings and the continued ability to benefit from the assets they've accumulated. On the death(s) of G1 (the primary beneficiaries of the 678 trust), generation-skipping transfer (GST) tax-exempt assets from the 678 trust pour over to the FAST. This pour-over can be achieved by G1 exercising a special power of appointment directing assets into the FAST, which also allows them to periodically adjust the amount of the pour-over. When funding a FAST, it's important to do so in a way that avoids potential GST tax liability.

Strengthen Family Cohesiveness

Whether a family realizes it or not, the patriarch and matriarch often act as the glue that holds the family together. Once they pass away, the dynamics of the family can shift drastically. By establishing a FAST, the family leaders are essentially creating a replacement glue that will assume the responsibility of fostering and nurturing family relations and of maintaining a family identity.

Shared values. Ensuring that the family has a clear

understanding of the patriarch's and matriarch's intentions and vision for the family can be crucial to the family's ability to work together as one unit. Creating a family mission statement can be a particularly impactful tool in this regard. According to an article from *The New York Times* entitled "The Stories That Bind Us," it's recommended that families craft a mission statement to preserve the core—similar to the way a large company often uses a mission statement to maintain its core values.[3] With a FAST, the trust agreement lays out the process to determine and preserve the family mission, beliefs, values and goals. Moreover, the drafting of the trust itself can serve as a way to initiate a conversation among the different generations of the family.

Family retreats. Another significant way the FAST promotes family relations is through the planning, coordination and financing of an annual family retreat. While conflicts and busy schedules are a typical part of any family, real problems emerge when there's no positive force pushing the family closer together acting as a balance against the stress. Family retreats can provide an ideal atmosphere for fellowship and the facilitation of meaningful and informative conversations regarding family affairs, all of which help to reinforce the stability and connectedness of the family. The distribution committee assumes responsibility for the planning of the family retreat, preparing activities and creating agendas for formal family meetings.

Family history. In addition to a clear family mission, a family's history can also serve as a unifier for the family. Furthermore, a knowledge of family history has been linked to higher self-esteem and better emotional health in children. Because a family's history is integral to maintaining a family identity, the distribution committee acts as a family historian, ensuring the documentation and dissemination of important aspects of the family's history. In practice, each distribution committee will carry out its role differently. Accordingly, overseeing the preservation of family history could include various tasks, including the safekeeping of family heirlooms, the creation of a written history of the family that's accessible to family members or the incorporation of family history lessons into family meetings or educational curriculum.

Maximize Heirs' Potential

In addition to strengthening the familial bond, expanded planning aims to prepare heirs to reach their maximum potential. Equipping a family to receive and successfully manage an inheritance is no small task, but it can be broken down into three parts: (1) education; (2) mentoring and practical experience; and (3) family philanthropy.

Education. The most effective way to approach the education of future heirs is to establish an education strategy. The strategy should be a dynamic, multi-faceted plan that aims to instill knowledge and wisdom in the next generation. Because creating and implementing this strategy can be an overwhelming task for any one family member, transferring that responsibility to a FAST can reap great rewards. Taking into account the ages, occupations and sophistication levels of the family members, as well as the characteristics of the family assets, the distribution committee determines what types of programs will be beneficial for preparing the family members to manage their inheritance and function as responsible members of society. Generally, an education plan will aim to cover basic topics: an understanding of family virtues, values and history; financial education; the ability to read and understand legal documents; the skills to make competent decisions in coordination with financial advisors; and the desire to participate in family meetings. A more sophisticated education plan would include additional curriculum related to the family business, as well as integrated family wealth management (financial planning, taxes, sustainable spend rates and market cycles). The distribution committee disseminates materials, schedules outside speakers to lead family meetings and ultimately ensures (and funds) the successful implementation of the family's education strategy.

Mentoring and practical experience. Overall, one of the primary benefits of the FAST is the message it sends to the family—specifically, that the family leaders aren't primarily interested in saving taxes or attaching strings to monetary gifts, but rather desire to empower the younger generations of the family. In this regard, the FAST aims to provide practical experience by serving as a mentor to beneficiaries, imparting wisdom instead of simply acting as a gatekeeper to the family wealth. The trust decision makers—the committee members—are in an ideal position to act as mentors to members of the younger generations.[4] For example, the investment committee could provide investment mentoring to the younger generations by meeting with each member annually to explain the investment decisions that have been made with respect to the trust. Some younger family members may need advice on how to be a better investor, while others may need advice on how to read a balance sheet. The mentor should

> In addition to education and
> practical experience, family
> philanthropy is vital to preparing
> heirs for their inheritance.

make resources available to the family member that will complement his unique learning needs.

The distribution committee grants practical experience to family members by making decisions regarding whether family funds should be gifted or loaned to a family member for entrepreneurial endeavors. Encouraging budding entrepreneurs not only teaches valuable business and money management skills, but also increases family interaction. It's important to note that the FAST itself doesn't gift or loan funds for entrepreneurial endeavors, but rather listens to proposals, advises and makes a recommendation as to whether family assets should be accessible to the applicant. The actual funds to be gifted or loaned should come from one of two places: if G1 is still living, then the funds should be drawn directly from them; if G1 is deceased, then the funds should come from a separate trust or family bank.

Under the structure of a FAST, the process of requesting money provides invaluable real-world experience. The FAST can implement protocols for the borrowing process, requiring the beneficiary to submit a lending request that summarizes the purposes of the loan, the proposed loan terms and how he plans to repay the money. Moreover, the distribution committee can maintain guidelines and limitations for the amounts that should be administered, with increasingly higher standards for those with a history for entrepreneurial failures or poor performance.

Family philanthropy. In addition to education and practical experience, family philanthropy is vital to preparing heirs for their inheritance. Charitable giving shows younger generations the value of helping others, and statistics show that the use of family philanthropy as a teaching tool is a determining factor in whether a family remains united. The FAST prepares the next generation to be leaders in the family's philanthropic activities by demonstrating how to give effectively and by allowing younger generations to select causes and take ownership of their own charitable investments. As with entrepreneurial development, no funds will be distributed directly from the FAST for charitable purposes. The distribution committee makes recommendations and approves charitable initiatives, while the actual charitable funds are drawn from the family's typical charitable gifting vehicle (for example, a family foundation or donor-advised fund).

Helping to preserve a family and prepare heirs for their inheritance may not be traditional estate-planning tasks, but there's a growing demand for this type of expanded planning. Our world is rapidly changing, and the estate-planning landscape has changed along with it. Clients are increasingly expecting more than just a set of documents from their estate planners, and those planners who refuse to adapt their practices, or move too slowly, will ultimately be left behind. The current state of estate planning may be one scenario where slow and steady won't win the race—it's time to act FAST.

Endnotes
1. Timothy J. Belber, Ian McDermott and John A. Warnick, "Innovate or Die," *Trusts & Estates* (September 2017), at p. 53.
2. This trust was jointly developed by Thomas Rogerson, a senior managing director and family wealth strategist at Wilmington Trust, NA and The Blum Firm, P.C.
3. Bruce Feiler, "The Stories that Bind Us," *The New York Times* (March 15, 2013).
4. James E. Hughes, Jr., "The Trustee as Mentor," *The Chase Journal* (Volume II, Issue 2, Spring 1998).

B: FAST Client Data
Questionnaire

Section 1 – Personal Information

Name Legal Name: _____

Date of Birth: _____ Cell Phone: _____

Spouse Legal Name: _____

Date of Birth: _____ Cell Phone: _____

Legal Address: _____

County: _____

Name of Trust:

_____

Default Name of Trust: The Family Advancement &

Sustainability Trust

Inventory of Assets To Initially Fund The Trust

Type Of Assets:

	<u>Client</u>	<u>Spouse</u>	<u>Joint</u>
Closely Held Business	_____	_____	_____
Income Producing Real Estate	_____	_____	_____
Personal Savings	_____	_____	_____
Investment Accounts	_____	_____	_____
Life Insurance	_____	_____	
New Policy Desired (Y / N)			

Section 2-A / Primary Beneficiaries

List of Living Beneficiaries:

Name: _____   Date of Birth:_____

Relationship: _____

Name: _____   Date of Birth:_____

Relationship: _____

Name: _____   Date of Birth:_____

Relationship: _____

Name: _____   Date of Birth:_____

Relationship: _____

Name: _____   Date of Birth:_____

Relationship: _____

Section 2-B / Disinherited Beneficiaries

Section 2-B is to identify bloodline relatives (if any) who are not to receive any portion of the Client's trust estate under any conditions. It is not necessary to identify the Client's distant relatives for purposes of this section. Also, do not enter names of in-laws because an in-law will never receive a portion of the estate unless identified as a beneficiary.

_____

_____

Section 3/Allocations

Select the appropriate provision for the share allocation(s) to the beneficiaries.

_____ The Annual Income ONLY shall be used to cover the expenses for the "Family Advancement & Sustainability" process for preparing heirs and/or the MTM Purposeful Family Forums (or any other program that is apropos for educating my heirs in the area of Family Values, Family Legacy, Family Gratitude, and Family Governance). If 100% of the income is not utilized for these services within the calendar year, the income shall be reinvested into the corpus of the trust to generate increased income in the future.

_____ Both Annual Income and/or Trust Corpus shall be used to cover the expenses for the "Family Advancement & Sustainability" process for preparing heirs and/or the MTM Purposeful Family Forums (or any other program that is apropos for educating my heirs in the area of Family Values, Family Legacy, Family Gratitude, and Family Governance). However, no more than _____ % of the corpus shall be withdrawn in any one calendar year. If 100% of the income is not utilized for these services within the calendar year, the income shall be reinvested into the corpus of the trust to generate increased income in the future.

_____ **Special Emergency Income Distribution Override Provision (optional):** If one of the living beneficiaries has an extraordinary financial emergency need, as determined by the distribution committee, the trustee can distribute up to _____ % of the income generated from the trust in that calendar year. This amount shall be subtracted from the funds allocated towards the Family Advancement & Sustainability process or Family Forums.

Section 4 / Fiduciaries

a) Trust Protector:

Name _____

Address: _____

E-Mail: _____

Mobile Phone: _____

b) Investment Committee Members:

Name _____

Address: _____

E-Mail: _____

Mobile Phone: _____

Name _____

Address: _____

E-Mail: _____

Mobile Phone: _____

Name _____

Address: _____

E-Mail: _____

Mobile Phone: _____

c)   Distribution Committee Members:

Name _____

Address: _____

E-Mail: _____

Mobile Phone: _____

Name _____

Address: _____

E-Mail: _____

Mobile Phone: _____

Name _____

Address: _____

E-Mail: _____

Mobile Phone: _____

Section 5 /Administrative Provisions

All properly drawn trusts must include directives (or administrative provisions & powers) for the trustee by the creator of the trust. In this Section we cover provisions that make up the directives normally given to the trustee.

The following is a brief explanation of each Administrative Provision:

5-1) This is a broadly defined fiduciary rule providing investment authority (and protection) to the fiduciary/Investment Committee under the Prudent Investor Act (PIA). The PIA essentially allows the Investment Committee to use a diversified portfolio of investment assets - from conservative to aggressive - as long as the choices meet an objective standard of prudence. Under the revised PIA rule, Investment Committee are not liable for the failure of any single investment unless it significantly impacts the entire trust investment portfolio. The PIA rule can be invoked in jurisdictions that have not yet codified the rule in their statutes. The PIA approach gives the trustee the latitude needed to optimize the trust income through use of the advanced investment opportunities available today.

5-2) This is a commonly used provision designed to prevent disgruntled beneficiaries from contesting the validity of the trust and depleting the trust estate through litigation. It requires that any beneficiary who unsuccessfully contests the trust forfeit his share. This simple provision has, undoubtedly, protected more than a few trust estates from the adverse consequences of contestation. Nevertheless, the Client may keep this statement out of the trust for any reason, personal or otherwise, if so desired.

5-3) This provision directs that a trust deemed Client's illegitimate descendants and their descendants as not being qualified as beneficiaries of the trust: illegitimate descendants are, therefore, intentionally omitted as beneficiaries. Illegitimate descendants are defined as those children (and their descendants) born to the Client out of wedlock. Stepchildren are also omitted, unless otherwise specified, and shall be deemed, for the purposes of this provision, as illegitimate children unless otherwise stated. Conversely, adopted children and their issue are treated as legitimate children, unless otherwise stated.

Administrative Provisions

Following are basic directives/provisions normally included in a Living Trust. Select Y (Yes) for those you want to include; select N (No) if not to be included:

Y / N   1) Any beneficiary who **unsuccessfully contests** your trust shall be disinherited and deemed as though he/she did not survive you and left now surviving children.

Y / N   2) Only **bloodline descendants** (born within matrimony) and legally adopted descendants may qualify to receive trust distributions – excluding descendants born outside of matrimony.

Section 6 / Beneficiary of Last Resort - Distributions to Charity

If at any such time in the future there are no surviving heirs to benefit from this trust, then the trust corpus shall be distributed to the charity and listed in this section.

QUALIFIED CHARITIES, for charitable estate tax deduction purposes, are generally IRC 501 (c)(3) organizations such as corporations, community chest funds, etc., organized and operated exclusively for religious, scientific, literary, or educational purposes; or for the purpose of the prevention of cruelty to children and/or animals, whose earnings do not inure to an individual and which do not attempt to influence legislation or politics. An annually updated list of recognized, qualified charities can be found in IRS "Publication 78," also known as the "Blue Book."

IRC 509(a) organizations, commonly referred to as Private Foundations, can also be listed as charitable beneficiaries. However, such organizations exist by exception rather than by definition in the Internal Revenue Code, and anyone making a transfer at death to such a charity expecting a charitable estate tax deduction should be wary of the complexities and frequent changes surrounding such organizations for gift and estate tax purposes.

Name of Family Foundation: _____

City: _____ State: _____

Share: _____% or $ _____

Name of Charity: _____

City: _____ State: _____

Share: _____% or $ _____

City: _____ State: _____

Share: _____% or $ _____

City: _____ State: _____

Share: _____% or $ _____

Additional Provisions – "Voice of the Client"

In your own words, please explain why you are making certain provisions within this trust. This is not part of the legal document but allows you to add "your voice" for your heirs to "hear."

_____

_____

_____

_____

_____

_____

_____

_____

Sample Language:

To the generations of The _____ family that will be the recipients of this trust:

As the grantor(s) of this trust, I (we) have strategically set aside a portion of our estate assets for the express purpose of providing the funds annually to finance the "More Than Money" education of our heirs.

Many families will donate funds to a university to educate strangers and we applaud such activities. However, we have elected to endow this trust for the benefit of you, our family.

I (we) have come to the conclusion that merely leaving valuables (money) to each of you without leaving an understanding of our family values can cause serious damage. It is our hope that by following a process for preparing each of you for the money (in the areas of Family Values, Family Gratitude, Family Legacy and Family Governance) that our family will be more closely knit, have a significant unified impact in this world and lead healthy and productive lives. By no means is there a magic pill that can be taken to ensure that these shall be accomplished, but if we are random with our approach, we will have random results. Hence, we seek to have a strategic plan to give our family the best possible chance for achieving these desired results.

Strong, solid family relationships don't just happen; there are critical elements that must be there for family ties to develop. When a relationship is built on a firm foundation it can withstand the hiccups of daily life and the unexpected moments of chaos. The main way that I(we) would like to accomplish this is through an Annual Family Forum. This is a family gathering that includes four elements; mutual respect, time for fun, constant encouragement and communicated love. It will be an opportunity to explore our "total" wealth — our personal, financial and social wealth.

I (we) are so confident that the time and effort we invest in our family's personal relationships will pay dividends for generations to come. I (we) hope that you will appreciate why I (we) have established this trust, so that from this point forward, our family will always be able to gather together, to grow together, without financial restraints.

I (we) are providing for you, our heirs, in this way because we love our family.

Blessings to all who shall become our family's future legacy.

_____

Grantor(s)

Administrative Trustee:

Argonne Trust Company, Inc.

4418 S. Technology Drive

Sioux Falls, SD 57106

Disclosures

The information in this booklet is intended to serve as a basis for discussion with financial, legal, tax and/or accounting advisors. It is not a substitute for competent advice from these advisors. The actual application of some of these concepts may be the practice of law and is the proper responsibility of an attorney. The application of other concepts may require the guidance of a tax or accounting advisor.

Although great effort has been taken to provide accurate numbers and explanations, the information in this report should not be relied upon for preparing tax returns or making investment decisions. Assumed rates of return are not in any way to be taken as guaranteed projections of actual returns from any recommended investment opportunity. If a numerical analysis is shown, the results are neither guarantees nor projections, and actual results may differ significantly. Any assumptions as to interest rates, rates of return, inflation, or other values are hypothetical and for illustrative purposes only. Rates of return shown are not indicative of any particular investment and will vary over time. Any reference to past performance is not indicative of future results and should not be taken as a guaranteed projection of actual returns from any recommended investment.

Biography

Monroe M. "Roey" Diefendorf, Jr.

Roey is a 50 year veteran wealth manager in Locust Valley, NY. He graduated from Deerfield Academy and Bucknell University where he received his degree in psychology. Roey has a Masters in Insurance from Georgia State University. He has completed the CLU, ChFC, RFC, CFP, CIMA and CAP designations over his career.

Roey has developed his national reputation in the "total" wealth management arena with the introduction of first two books "3 Dimensional Wealth: A Radically Sane Perspective On Wealth Management" and "A Better Way: Using Purposeful Trusts To Preserve Values & Valuables In Perpetuity". In addition, he has authored, "South Dakota, USA – 57106: The Preferred Jurisdiction For Your Trust Needs", "3D Wealth: A New Paradigm In Planning – How To Capture Your Client's Values In A Trust", "Tax Sheltered Impact Investing: Through The Monroe Insurance Dedicated Funds" and "US Trusts for Foreign Nationals: South Dakota – The One & Only."

Roey has also co-authored "Private Placement Life Insurance: A Sophisticated Investment Solution for High Net Worth Investors" and "Private Placement Variable Annuity: A Sophisticated Investment Solution for High Net Worth Investors" with Gerald Nowotny, JD, LLM.

Roey is the Chief Executive Officer of 3 Dimensional Wealth Advisory, LLC (formerly Diefendorf Capital Planning Associates), More Than Money Family Office, LLC and MTM Advisory, LLC. He founded both Argonne Trust Company, Inc. (SD) and the Monroe Insurance Dedicated Funds (DE) bringing values-based solutions to the domestic PPLI marketplace as well as the traditional insurance arena.

Along with Shawn Barberis, JD, Roey has created "More Than Money 360" (MTM360), which is the digital platform for "total" wealth managers to help their clients prepare their heirs for the money.

Shawn and Roey are the principals of MTM Educational Resources (501c3), dedicated to bringing the message of "more than money" to advisors and families.

Shawn T. Barberis

Shawn is an attorney who founded Premier Planning Group in 2001, serving as Managing Partner, an independent financial services firm with several offices up and

down the East Coast. After several exceptionally good years, his entrepreneurial spirit finally got the best of him and he decided to move away from that partnership and start Aspida360, a technology firm for preparing heirs. Shawn knew the key to acting in his client's best interests was to create a platform to define, protect, perpetuate and communicate family legacy, traditions, philanthropy, life experiences and core values while mitigating the high rate of wealth transfer failure.

For More Information:

MTM Educational Resources, Inc.

4481 S. Technology Dr., Sioux Falls, SD 57106

Made in the USA
Middletown, DE
29 May 2020